Holes the Crickets Have Eaten in Blankets

This pamphlet was made possible
with the generous support of Karen Trueheart,
Jane Moress Schuster and William Hoskin

Holes the Crickets Have Eaten in Blankets

A sequence of poems
by

Robert Bly

Boa Editions, Ltd. ∞ Rochester, New York ∞ 1997

LC #: 97–72086
ISBN: 1–880238–58–6 paper
ISBN: 1–880238–57–7 specially bound, limited

First Edition
97 98 99 00   7 6 5 4 3 2 1

Publications by BOA Editions, Ltd.—
a not-for-profit corporation under section 501 (c) (3)
of the United States Internal Revenue Code—
are supported by grants from
the Literature Program of the New York State Council on the Arts,
and the Literature Program of the National Endowment for the Arts,
the Lannan Foundation, the Sonia Raiziss Giop Charitable Foundation,
the Eric Mathieu King Fund of The Academy of American Poets,
as well as from the Rochester Area Community Foundation Community Arts Fund
administered by the Arts & Cultural Council for Greater Rochester,
the County of Monroe, NY,
and from many individual supporters.

Frontispiece: *Day*, plate VI from *Dreams*, (1891), by Odilon Redon.
Lithograph printed in black, composition: 8$\frac{1}{4}$ x 6$\frac{1}{8}$" (21 x 15.5 cm.).
The Museum of Modern Art, New York. Lillie P. Bliss Collection.
Photograph © 1997 The Museum of Modern Art, New York.

"The Bear and the Man" copyright © 1997 by Robert Bly, reprinted from
Morning Poems, by Robert Bly, with the permission of HarperCollins.

David Ignatow, "Three in Transition" from *Against the Evidence:
Selected Poems 1934–1994* © 1993 by David Ignatow, Wesleyan University
Press by permission of University Press of New England.

BOA Logo: Mirko

BOA Editions, Ltd.
Alexandra Northrop, Chair
A. Poulin, Jr., President & Founder (1976–1996)
260 East Avenue
Rochester, NY 14604

These poems are published in memory of Samuel Ray,
who was Ruth Bly's and David Ray's son,
and my dear stepson.

CONTENTS

∞

ON ASSATEAGUE ISLAND

November evening
Makes dusky
The dunes,
Gray sand
Deepens
And goes farther away.
I seldom speak
My grief,
I think it under
The water,
Turn it over
And over.
Herds of wild ponies
Leave hoofmarks
Up and down
This long
Forty mile island.
Some people respect
Only light
Streaming in
From distant stars.
I grieve
In Milky Ways
And speak
In single stars.
I keep this grief
To myself.
My words
Are a single
Horse,

With low belly,
Alone.

AFTER YOUR DEATH

Sam, now where have you gone?
I held you often on my knees,
My arms circling you, and we
Were friends, helping each other.

In winter you worked late
Into the night, all one week,
Working Robert Frost's words
Into a cypress root for me.

Now the root speaks the words
You loved so well.
"Almost like a call to come in
To the dark and lament."

MY DREAM

I saw you nearly at dawn in a bath,
Naked in hot water, with your head thrown back.

"I was in the house of books, being washed.
It was in water almost too hot
For the three of us, being washed."

You added: "Dry me with your breath
For intense breath is prayer.
And it loosens the bonds of water."

DECEMBER

Wind blows from the lake; the ponderous
Spruce boughs agree to talk about it.
But it's unlikely they will change their mind.

We turn our backs for a week in December,
We go to the city, never think of the snow at all,
And when we return the lake is frozen.

You dreamt last night that Sam put
The upper part of his body and his head
Down on the coffee table and wept.

THE BEAR AND THE MAN

Suppose there were a bear and a man. The bear
Knows his kin—old pebbles, fifty-five-
Gallon barrels, pine trees in the moonlight,
Abandoned down jackets; and the man approaches warily—

He's read Tolstoy, knows a few symphonies.
That's about it. Each has lost a son. The bear's
Killed by a trap, the man's killed by a bear.
That boy was partly drunk, alone in the woods.

The bear puts out black claws firmly on earth.
He's not dumb. Skinned, he's like a man. People
Say that both bears and men receive a signal
Coming from far up there, near the North Pole.

LAKE SEBAGO, MAINE

The undersides of birch leaves seem so frail—
They turn their backs to wind and hurry away.

A man puts his foot on a bent birch near the cliff.
And the birch trunk sways under his foot.

The wind darkens the lake with cannibal thoughts.
The foam of each wave speaks, argues, and is gone.

The sandy water moves its bitter plans to land.
Death has won some argument with the little shells.

HOLES IN OUR SPEECH

After having left blankets out on the grass all night,
I notice holes the crickets have eaten in the wool.
A man and a woman stretched out asleep
Will find the cold slipping in through those holes.

What we fail to see enters during the night.
It frightens the red-haired woman who brings
Her grey-haired lover to the Emergency door.
At the funeral people say: "How could we have missed it?"

Men and women build a house and live there,
And the roof falls if they let a single board go.
What we do not care to say fills the mouth
When we fail to speak a certain essential word.

VISITING A CLIFF IN SMÅLAND

*Persons in Viking times arranged on this Swedish cliff
a group of stones in the shape of a long-ship.*

Some few dandelions already turned into old men's heads
Stand around this ritual boat whose gunwales are stone.

This growling ground must have been sweet to the rowdy men
And women who woke, saved from glowering hags in their sleep.

Dreams were more frightening then—God appeared sometimes
At night as a dog with one leg, a Hag's son, or a man-eater.

Men clambered into the boat, they slept, they snored, then
The Hag pulled them down out of their seats into the sea.

"Oh yes," the sailors say, "we are glad that doesn't happen
To us. We are safe here eighty feet off the sea."

THE ABANDONED HERMIT'S CABIN

Even though leaves die in fall, it's clear that birds
Still want to live. The wren weaves her nest,
The wild waters refuse all sober tasks,
The boy and girl hold new roses when they marry.

We go on believing that we remain
Welcome here; and our tongues keep wanting
To speak the words *he* and *she* and *our*—
Those sounds to which our throats remain loyal.

But this world we cling to is only an unroofed
Hermit's cabin—the hermit long dead, the stove
Turned over, stovepipes down, door
Hinges pulled out, quilts and dishes scattered.

ATTEMPTING TO ANSWER
DAVID IGNATOW'S QUESTION

> *I wish I understood the beauty*
> *in leaves falling. To whom*
> *are we beautiful*
> *as we go?*

We are beautiful to the Mother as we go.
There are mysterious roads in jade that
Old men follow,
Routes that migratory birds walk on,
The circle dances
Iron filings do,
The things we cannot say.
Salmon find their way to old beds;
Sleeping bodies are not alone.

FROST AND HIS ENEMIES

When Robert Frost set down a poetic whim,
The darkness with open mouth went looking for him.

Flowers love sun; but larvae, even at noon,
In their murky pond are excited by the moon!

When a foot in a marsh works to get free,
Water fills up the hole immediately.

When Frost sat down to get a poem right,
He was a sandy place open to night.

He wanted to see white, even if it were a birch,
Or a patch of snow or the steeple of a church.

COLOPHON

Holes the Crickets Have Eaten in Blankets,
a sequence of poems by Robert Bly,
has been issued in a first printing of 3,000 copies,
of which 2,925 trade copies are bound in wrappers.
Seventy-five copies are bound in quarter-cloth and French papers
over boards, numbered "1" through "75," and signed by the poet.

The text was set using Goudy fonts
by Richard Foerster, York Beach, Maine.
The cover was designed by
Geri McCormick, Rochester, New York.
Manufacturing was by Midtown Printing & Graphics,
Rochester, New York.